AI in High-Risk Industries

Healthcare, Finance, & Law Enforcement

By Joe Correa

Published by Live Stronger Faster

This book is for educational and informational purposes only. The author and publisher are not engaged in rendering legal, financial, or other professional advice. Readers should consult a qualified professional before making any financial decisions.

First Edition

Table of Contents

Overview

The moment artificial intelligence leaves the realm of recommendation engines and entertainment and enters hospitals, banks, police departments, courtrooms, and battlefields, it stops being a neutral technology and becomes a force that directly governs human lives. In high-risk industries, an algorithm does not simply predict what movie you will watch or which product you might buy—it decides who receives a life-saving treatment, who gets approved for a mortgage, who is flagged as a criminal suspect, and who may be targeted in a military operation. These decisions carry irreversible consequences, which means that in these environments, AI is no longer just software; it becomes an authority. This book begins from that reality: when machines are allowed to shape human destiny, the standards for ethics, governance, transparency, and accountability must be higher than anywhere else. A flawed recommendation on a shopping website can be annoying, but a flawed diagnosis, credit decision, or use-of-force prediction can destroy lives, families, and entire communities. That is why high-risk AI must be governed differently, and why this book exists.

High-risk industries are unique because the margin for error is near zero. A medical AI that misclassifies cancer does not simply make a mistake; it creates a death sentence. A credit algorithm that embeds hidden bias does not just produce a bad number; it can lock families out of homeownership and wealth for generations. A policing system that predicts crime based on flawed data does not merely analyze trends; it can justify harassment, surveillance, and incarceration. A military AI that misidentifies a target does not generate a technical glitch; it can end human lives and trigger geopolitical catastrophe. When we allow machines to operate at this level, we are no longer talking about productivity tools—we are talking about delegated power. This book treats AI in these sectors as a form of institutional authority, and therefore subject to the same moral, legal, and democratic constraints as any human institution.

What makes this moment especially dangerous is that many of these systems already exist, yet most citizens do not know they are being used. Algorithms already decide which patients are prioritized in hospitals, which borrowers get better interest rates, which neighborhoods are patrolled more heavily, and which travelers are flagged at borders. The automation is quiet, invisible, and often shielded behind claims of proprietary technology. This creates a new kind of power imbalance: people are judged, scored, categorized, and acted upon by machines they cannot see, question, or challenge. In high-risk industries, this lack of transparency is not just unethical—it is fundamentally incompatible with democracy and human rights. If people cannot understand or contest the systems that govern their lives, they no longer truly live under the rule of law, but under the rule of code.

Healthcare is one of the clearest examples of this transformation. AI systems are now used to analyze medical images, predict disease, allocate hospital resources, and even recommend treatment plans. While these tools promise faster diagnoses and more efficient care, they also introduce profound ethical hazards. A model trained on biased or incomplete data may misdiagnose minorities, women, or the elderly. A hospital that relies too heavily on algorithmic triage may unknowingly deny care to those who need it most. Worse, patients often have no idea that a machine influenced their diagnosis or treatment. This book does not argue against medical AI; it argues for medical AI that is transparent, accountable, auditable, and always subordinate to human judgment. In a world where algorithms can influence life-or-death decisions, blind trust is not innovation—it is negligence.

Finance is another arena where AI now wields enormous power. Credit scoring, fraud detection, loan approvals, insurance pricing, and investment decisions are increasingly driven by automated systems. These algorithms can process millions of data points and identify patterns that humans cannot, but they can also replicate and amplify existing inequalities. A biased credit model does not merely discriminate once—it does so systematically, at massive scale. A flawed fraud-detection system can freeze accounts, deny access to funds, or label innocent people as criminals. When financial AI goes wrong, it does not just hurt individual customers; it destabilizes trust in the entire economic system. This book will show why financial AI must be governed with the same seriousness as banks themselves, because in practice, many algorithms now function as financial institutions.

Law enforcement and border control represent perhaps the most troubling uses of high-risk AI. Predictive policing, facial recognition, and risk-scoring systems promise efficiency and objectivity, but in reality they often operate as opaque surveillance machines. When police rely on algorithms to decide where to patrol, who to stop, and who to investigate, they risk outsourcing civil liberties to software. When facial recognition systems misidentify people, the result can be wrongful arrests, detentions, or worse. When border algorithms label someone as high risk, that person may never know why they were denied entry or subjected to scrutiny. In these contexts, AI does not just assist human authority—it reshapes it. This book treats these systems as digital forms of policing and immigration control, which means they must be subject to constitutional, legal, and human rights safeguards.

Nowhere are the stakes higher than in military and defense applications of AI. Autonomous weapons, battlefield decision systems, and algorithmic targeting tools are no longer science fiction—they are real and rapidly evolving. These systems promise faster reactions and strategic advantages, but they also create terrifying risks. An AI that misclassifies a civilian as a combatant can trigger lethal force without human oversight. A swarm of autonomous drones can escalate conflicts faster than any human commander could intervene. When war is delegated to machines, accountability becomes dangerously blurred. Who is responsible when an algorithm decides if a life should be taken or not? The programmer, the commander, the manufacturer, or the machine itself? This book insists that there must never be a moral or legal vacuum around AI-driven violence, because the cost of ambiguity in warfare is measured in human lives.

Across all of these industries, one pattern repeats: organizations deploy powerful AI systems faster than they build the governance structures to control them. Hospitals, banks, police departments, and defense agencies are adopting algorithms because they promise efficiency, cost savings, and competitive advantage, but too often they do so without fully understanding the ethical, legal, and social risks. This creates what can only be called algorithmic recklessness—a willingness to let machines make high-impact decisions without adequate oversight. The purpose of this book is to close that gap by providing a clear, practical framework for understanding how AI must be governed in environments where mistakes are not just inconvenient but catastrophic.

This volume sits at the heart of the AI Ethics & Governance series because high-risk industries are where theory meets reality. The principles explored in earlier books—fairness, transparency, privacy, accountability, and governance—are not abstract here. They determine who gets medical care, who receives financial opportunity, who is free, and who lives or dies. In these sectors, ethical AI is not a luxury or a branding exercise; it is a moral obligation and a legal necessity. By the end of this book, you will understand why high-risk AI must be treated like critical infrastructure, governed with rigor, and designed with human dignity at its core, because in the end, the true test of artificial intelligence is not how powerful it becomes, but how responsibly we choose to use it.

Chapter 1

Medical AI & The Risks in Human Life

Medical artificial intelligence represents one of the most powerful and dangerous transformations in modern history because it places machine intelligence directly between doctors and patients. Unlike AI used for marketing or entertainment, medical AI interacts with human biology, disease, and mortality. Every prediction, diagnosis, and treatment recommendation produced by an algorithm has the potential to change the trajectory of a human life. When a machine classifies a tumor as benign instead of malignant, or recommends a drug that a patient's genetics cannot tolerate, the consequences are not abstract—they are measured in suffering, survival, and death. This is why medical AI must be treated as a regulated medical device, not just a software tool, and why ethics, governance, and accountability are as important as accuracy.

At its core, medical AI works by analyzing enormous volumes of health data—medical images, lab results, genetic information, clinical notes, wearable device data, and population health records—to identify patterns that humans cannot see. These systems are trained using machine learning models that learn correlations between symptoms, test results, and outcomes. In theory, this allows them to detect disease earlier, personalize treatment, and improve efficiency. In practice, however, these systems inherit the strengths and weaknesses of the data they are trained on. If a dataset overrepresents certain populations and underrepresents others, the AI will produce skewed predictions. A system trained mostly on data from white male patients, for example, may fail to accurately diagnose conditions in women or minority groups, even if it performs extremely well in controlled testing environments.

Bias in medical AI is particularly dangerous because it is often invisible to clinicians. A doctor may assume that an algorithm is objective, not realizing that it reflects historical inequalities in healthcare access, diagnostic practices, and treatment outcomes. If underserved communities have received less care in the past, the data will suggest they need less care in the future, even if their medical needs are greater. This creates a feedback loop where AI reinforces and amplifies existing disparities. Without intentional oversight, medical AI can quietly encode racism, sexism, and socioeconomic bias into healthcare systems that already struggle with fairness.

Another critical risk in medical AI is explainability. Many advanced models, especially deep learning systems, function as black boxes. They produce highly accurate predictions but cannot clearly explain how those predictions were made. In a medical setting, this is deeply problematic. Doctors are ethically and legally required to understand the basis of a diagnosis or treatment recommendation. Patients have the right to informed consent, which means they must be able to understand why a particular medical decision is being made. If an AI cannot explain why it recommends surgery instead of medication, or why it flags one patient as high risk and not another, it undermines both clinical judgment and patient autonomy.

Regulators around the world are beginning to recognize that medical AI must be governed like any other medical technology. In the United States, the Food and Drug Administration increasingly treats AI systems as medical devices that require approval, monitoring, and post-deployment oversight. In Europe, medical AI falls under both health regulations and the AI Act's high-risk classification. These frameworks acknowledge that once software influences diagnosis or treatment, it becomes part of the clinical decision-making process and must be held to the same standards of safety, reliability, and accountability as drugs or surgical tools. This means validation, audit trails, continuous monitoring, and the ability to detect when a model's performance drifts over time.

One of the most overlooked dangers in medical AI is automation bias. When clinicians see a confident recommendation from a machine, they may subconsciously trust it more than their own judgment, even when it is wrong. This is especially true in busy hospitals where staff are overworked and under pressure to make rapid decisions. If an AI system consistently appears accurate, doctors may begin to defer to it without questioning its outputs. When this happens, errors become harder to detect, and responsibility becomes blurred. Was it the doctor's fault for following the machine, or the developer's fault for designing it? Effective governance must ensure that humans remain in the loop, with clear authority and responsibility for final decisions.

Medical data privacy is another pillar of ethical AI in healthcare. AI systems require vast amounts of patient data to function, but that data is deeply personal and highly sensitive. Genetic profiles, mental health records, reproductive history, and chronic conditions can be exploited if misused or breached. Hospitals and AI vendors must implement strict data governance, encryption, access controls, and consent mechanisms to ensure that patients understand how their information is being used. Ethical medical AI does not treat patient data as a free resource; it treats it as a form of human dignity that must be protected.

There is also the issue of who benefits from medical AI. Many advanced systems are developed by large technology companies that may prioritize profit over public health. If proprietary algorithms are used to guide care, but their inner workings are kept secret, hospitals and patients are forced to trust corporations without transparency. This creates a dangerous imbalance of power, where life-saving decisions depend on technology that cannot be independently audited. Ethical governance requires that high-risk medical AI be subject to external review, regulatory scrutiny, and meaningful oversight, even when it is owned by private companies.

The future of medical AI will not be determined by technology alone, but by the rules and values we impose on it. We can choose a future where algorithms enhance human doctors, improve outcomes, and reduce suffering, or we can drift into a system where patients are managed by opaque machines that optimize for efficiency rather than compassion. The difference lies in governance. By demanding transparency, fairness, accountability, and human oversight, society can ensure that medical AI becomes a tool for healing rather than a source of harm. In high-risk environments like healthcare, ethical AI is not optional—it is the foundation of trust.

*"The Algorithm That Knew Too Much"***

Dr. Elena Morales had always trusted data, but she had never trusted it blindly. As a senior oncologist at St. Raphael Medical Center, she had seen too many miracles and too many tragedies to believe that numbers alone could tell the whole story of a human body. Still, when the hospital installed a new AI diagnostic system called Aesclepius, she was cautiously optimistic. The machine could analyze scans, blood tests, and genetic profiles in seconds, producing treatment recommendations that once took teams of specialists days to reach. To the hospital board, it was a revolution. To Elena, it was a powerful tool that needed careful hands.

The first weeks went smoothly. Aesclepius caught early-stage cancers that radiologists had missed and suggested therapies that worked better than standard protocols. Doctors began to rely on it more and more, and administrators praised its efficiency. Then one afternoon, Elena met a patient named Rosa Delgado. Rosa was a fifty-two-year-old woman with vague symptoms—fatigue, pain, and unexplained weight loss. Her scans were unclear, but Elena's instincts told her something was wrong. When she ran Rosa's data through Aesclepius, the system returned a low-risk score and recommended no further testing. According to the algorithm, Rosa was fine.

Elena hesitated. She had learned to respect the machine, but something about Rosa's case felt different. Against protocol, she ordered additional tests. A week later, the results came back: aggressive ovarian cancer, already spreading. If Elena had followed the AI's recommendation, Rosa might have gone home untreated until it was too late. When Elena confronted the hospital's AI team, they were shocked. The system had an accuracy rate of over 95 percent. "It must be an outlier," they said. But Elena knew that behind every outlier was a person.

Digging deeper, Elena discovered that Aesclepius had been trained mostly on data from men and younger patients. Symptoms that presented differently in middle-aged women were underweighted in its calculations. The machine was not malicious–it was blind to what it had never learned. When Elena presented this to the board, they were uneasy. Admitting the flaw would mean admitting liability. It could mean lawsuits, regulatory scrutiny, and damaged reputation. Some suggested quietly fixing the model and moving on.

Elena refused. Rosa deserved the truth, and so did every patient who would ever be evaluated by the system. She pushed for a full audit and public disclosure. The process was painful and expensive, but it forced the hospital to rebuild Aesclepius with more diverse data, stronger oversight, and clear rules that doctors, not machines, had the final say. Rosa began treatment, and though her battle was hard, she had a chance she would never have had if the algorithm had been trusted without question.

Months later, Elena watched as the updated system went live. It was better now—not just more accurate, but more humble. It flagged uncertainty instead of hiding it and asked for human review when cases fell outside its confidence. Elena smiled. The algorithm still knew a great deal, but it no longer pretended to know everything. And in a place where lives hung in the balance, that made all the difference.

Chapter 2

Credit & Lending in the World of AI

Artificial intelligence has quietly become one of the most powerful forces in modern finance because it now decides who is worthy of credit, on what terms, and at what cost. Every mortgage approval, personal loan, credit card limit, and insurance premium increasingly depends on algorithms that evaluate risk, income stability, behavioral patterns, and thousands of hidden variables. In theory, this creates efficiency and removes human bias, but in reality it often replaces visible human judgment with invisible machine judgment that is far harder to challenge. In high-risk financial systems, AI does not merely predict outcomes—it allocates opportunity, and when it gets that wrong, it can lock people out of housing, education, entrepreneurship, and long-term wealth.

Modern credit AI systems go far beyond traditional credit scores. They ingest transaction histories, employment data, spending behavior, social signals, device metadata, and even geolocation patterns to build a profile of each borrower. These models attempt to predict not only whether someone will repay a loan, but how profitable they will be for a lender over time. This means that borrowers are no longer evaluated only on past behavior, but on predicted future value to a financial institution. While this allows lenders to expand credit to people who might not qualify under older systems, it also introduces new forms of discrimination that are harder to detect and regulate.

One of the greatest dangers of AI-driven lending is proxy discrimination. Even when algorithms do not explicitly use protected characteristics like race, gender, or age, they can infer them from other data points such as zip codes, education histories, purchasing patterns, or employment gaps. This allows discriminatory outcomes to occur without any obvious discriminatory inputs. A model may deny a loan to a borrower not because of creditworthiness, but because people who look statistically similar to them were historically denied credit. In this way, AI can fossilize the inequalities of the past and project them into the future at massive scale.

Transparency is another major challenge in AI-based lending. Many financial institutions cannot fully explain why a particular applicant was approved or rejected, because the decision was produced by a complex machine-learning model. Yet lending laws around the world require lenders to provide adverse action notices explaining why credit was denied. If an algorithm cannot explain itself, the institution may be violating consumer protection laws without even realizing it.

This creates legal, financial, and reputational risks for banks and fintech companies that deploy black-box models without sufficient oversight.

The use of alternative data in credit scoring introduces both opportunity and danger. On one hand, it can allow people with thin or no credit histories to access loans by demonstrating reliability through rent payments, utility bills, or bank account activity. On the other hand, it can turn everyday life into a surveillance system, where every purchase, every late payment, and every behavioral signal is used to judge financial worthiness. When combined with AI, this data can create hyper-detailed profiles that individuals have no ability to inspect, correct, or escape. Financial freedom becomes conditional on algorithmic approval.

Regulators are beginning to treat AI in lending as a high-risk technology. In the United States, the Equal Credit Opportunity Act and Fair Credit Reporting Act impose strict rules on how decisions must be made and explained. In Europe, financial AI is covered by both consumer protection law and the AI Act's high-risk system requirements. These frameworks demand accuracy, fairness, auditability, and the ability to contest automated decisions. Yet many lenders deploy AI models that were designed for prediction, not for legal defensibility, creating a growing gap between what the law requires and what the technology provides.

Another overlooked risk is model drift. Economic conditions change, consumer behavior shifts, and financial stress rises and falls. An AI model trained on pre-pandemic data may make dangerously inaccurate predictions in a post-pandemic economy. If lenders do not continuously monitor and retrain their systems, they can unintentionally tighten or loosen credit in ways that destabilize both borrowers and the broader economy. In extreme cases, poorly governed AI can contribute to credit bubbles, systemic risk, and financial crises.

Human oversight remains essential in AI-driven lending. While machines are excellent at identifying patterns, they cannot understand context, hardship, or nuance in the way people can. A borrower recovering from illness, a small business rebuilding after a disaster, or a family navigating temporary financial stress may appear risky to an algorithm but deserving of flexibility in reality. Ethical financial systems require that automated decisions be reviewable, challengeable, and reversible by human experts who understand the real-world impact.

Ultimately, AI in credit and lending will shape the future of economic opportunity. If governed responsibly, it can expand access, reduce costs, and make finance more inclusive. If left unchecked, it can create a world where financial destiny is determined by invisible models that no one can question. High-risk financial AI must therefore be transparent, fair, and accountable, because in a society built on credit, algorithmic decisions determine who gets to build a life and who is left behind.

"The Loan the Algorithm Refused"

Marcus Reed had built his life from nothing. After growing up in a neighborhood where opportunity was scarce, he had spent years working two jobs, saving every extra dollar, and finally launching a small construction business. When the demand for renovations surged, Marcus needed capital to hire workers and buy equipment. He walked into a sleek digital bank, confident that his spotless payment history and growing revenue would secure the loan.

Instead, the AI system rejected him in less than two seconds.

The screen flashed a polite message: *Application Denied. Risk Profile Does Not Meet Criteria.* No explanation, no appeal, no human contact. Marcus was stunned. His business was profitable. His credit score was solid. When he tried another lender, the result was the same. Different company, same algorithmic verdict. It was as if an invisible wall had been erected around him. Determined to understand what was happening, Marcus contacted a consumer advocacy group. They discovered that the AI models used by many lenders heavily weighted factors like neighborhood location and cash-flow volatility. Marcus lived in a historically underfunded zip code, and his income, though growing, fluctuated month to month like most small businesses. The algorithm saw this as danger, even though it was the very pattern of an entrepreneur on the rise.

A lawyer helped Marcus file a formal complaint. The bank was forced to audit its system. The investigation revealed that thousands of minority-owned businesses were being rejected at higher rates, not because of actual risk, but because the model associated their demographic and geographic data with past defaults. The AI was not evaluating Marcus—it was evaluating a statistical shadow of him.

After months of pressure, the bank revised its model and created a human review process for borderline cases. Marcus reapplied. This time, a loan officer looked at his real financials, his contracts, and his business plan. He was approved.

As Marcus hired new workers and expanded his company, he realized how close he had come to being erased by a machine. The algorithm had almost written his future, not because he was unworthy, but because it could not see his potential. And in a world where credit is power, being invisible to AI is one of the greatest risks of all.

Chapter 3

Policing Algorithms That Assist Decision-Making

Policing algorithms represent one of the most profound and dangerous shifts in the relationship between the state and its citizens because they move the power of suspicion, surveillance, and enforcement from human judgment to machine calculation. When artificial intelligence is used to predict crime, identify suspects, or allocate police resources, it does more than optimize operations—it shapes who is watched, who is stopped, and who is treated as a threat. In high-risk environments like law enforcement, AI does not simply assist decision-making; it actively constructs reality by deciding where danger is assumed to exist. This makes policing algorithms not just tools, but engines of social control.

Predictive policing systems analyze historical crime data, arrest records, 911 calls, and other inputs to forecast where crime is likely to occur and who is likely to be involved. These models claim to remove human bias by relying on data, but in practice they encode and amplify the biases already present in the justice system. If certain neighborhoods have been over-policed in the past, they will generate more crime data, which in turn causes the algorithm to send more police to those same neighborhoods. This creates a self-reinforcing cycle where communities are trapped in a feedback loop of surveillance, stops, and arrests, regardless of their actual behavior.

One of the most dangerous features of policing algorithms is their aura of objectivity. Officers, judges, and policymakers may assume that a machine-generated risk score or hotspot map is neutral and scientific, even when it is based on deeply flawed data. This can lead to decisions that would never be accepted if they came from a human being. An officer might hesitate to target someone based on a gut feeling, but will act confidently when an algorithm labels a person or location as high risk. In this way, AI can launder bias through mathematics, making discriminatory outcomes appear legitimate.

Facial recognition technology introduces an even more alarming layer of risk. These systems attempt to identify individuals by comparing images from cameras to large databases of photos. Numerous studies have shown that facial recognition performs far worse on women, people of color, and young or elderly faces. In a policing context, this means that certain groups are far more likely to be misidentified as suspects. When a false match leads to an arrest, detention, or use of force, the consequences are immediate and severe.

Unlike a human witness, an algorithm does not feel doubt, fear, or moral hesitation—it simply outputs a match.

Legal accountability becomes murky when AI is used in policing. If an officer acts on an algorithmic recommendation that turns out to be wrong, who is responsible? The officer who followed the system, the department that purchased it, or the company that built it? Many vendors claim that their algorithms are proprietary and cannot be fully disclosed, which makes independent auditing nearly impossible. This creates a dangerous gap between technological power and legal oversight, allowing high-risk systems to operate without meaningful checks and balances.

Policing algorithms also raise profound privacy concerns. Surveillance cameras, license plate readers, social media monitoring, and phone metadata are increasingly fed into AI systems that map people's movements, relationships, and behavior. Even individuals who have committed no crime can find themselves flagged, tracked, or profiled based on statistical associations. This erodes the presumption of innocence and creates a society where everyone is a potential suspect in a vast digital dragnet.

From an ethical standpoint, the use of AI in law enforcement must be governed by the same principles that guide the justice system: fairness, due process, proportionality, and accountability. Automated systems should never be the sole basis for stops, arrests, or charges. Individuals must have the right to know when an algorithm influenced a decision about them and to challenge that decision in court. Without these safeguards, policing AI becomes a form of algorithmic authoritarianism.

The future of public safety depends on how we choose to use these technologies. AI can help allocate resources, identify patterns of violence, and even prevent harm, but only if it is carefully constrained and transparently governed. In high-risk environments like policing, the goal must not be to replace human judgment with machines, but to ensure that technology serves justice rather than undermines it. Without strict oversight, policing algorithms risk turning data into destiny and suspicion into policy.

"The Red Zone"

Officer Daniel Wright had been on the force for twelve years when the new system arrived. It was called Sentinel, and it promised to predict crime before it happened. Every morning, officers received a digital map filled with glowing red zones—neighborhoods the algorithm believed were most likely to see criminal activity that day. Daniel had grown used to trusting his instincts, but the department now expected him to trust the map more. At first, it seemed to work. Patrols in the red zones led to more stops, more searches, and more arrests. Commanders praised the data. But Daniel began to notice something unsettling. The same streets were always red. The same faces were always stopped. Kids he had seen grow up were being questioned again and again, even when they had done nothing wrong.

One evening, Daniel stopped a teenager named Jamal because Sentinel flagged him as high risk. Jamal was walking home from school, carrying a backpack full of books. The algorithm said his location and social network made him likely to be involved in a crime. Daniel searched him and found nothing. Jamal's eyes burned with quiet anger. "Why me?" he asked. Daniel had no answer.

Weeks later, Jamal was arrested after a facial recognition system matched him to a robbery suspect. Daniel knew the boy wasn't capable of it. He reviewed the footage and saw that the image was blurry and the match uncertain, but the system insisted. Jamal spent three nights in jail before the mistake was discovered.

Daniel finally understood what Sentinel was doing. It wasn't finding criminals—it was creating them by treating certain people as suspects until something went wrong. He filed a report, risking his career. The department launched an investigation. The red zones were red not because of crime, but because they had been red before. As Sentinel was quietly scaled back, Daniel realized that justice could never be automated. A machine could calculate risk, but it could not see a human being. And in a world where algorithms decided who belonged in the red zone, that difference mattered more than ever.

Chapter 4

AI Border Control Implications

Artificial intelligence has become one of the most powerful forces shaping modern border control because it now determines who is allowed to enter a country, who is flagged for additional scrutiny, and who is denied freedom of movement altogether. In an age of global travel, migration, and geopolitical instability, governments increasingly rely on AI systems to process millions of travelers, asylum seekers, and visa applicants. These systems promise efficiency and security, but they also introduce unprecedented risks to human rights, due process, and personal liberty. When an algorithm labels a person as high risk, the consequences can include detention, deportation, family separation, or permanent exclusion from opportunity.

Modern border AI systems combine biometric data, travel histories, financial records, social media activity, and intelligence databases to build risk profiles for individuals. Facial recognition cameras scan airports and checkpoints, linking faces to vast databases of images. Automated systems analyze passports, visas, and flight patterns to detect anomalies. In theory, this allows authorities to identify genuine threats quickly. In practice, it creates a massive surveillance infrastructure that treats every traveler as a data subject and every movement as a potential risk signal.

One of the most serious ethical dangers of border AI is error. Facial recognition systems are known to have higher error rates for women, darker-skinned individuals, and people from underrepresented populations. When these systems are used at borders, a false match can mean hours or days of detention, missed connections, or denial of entry into a country. For asylum seekers and refugees, a single mistaken risk score can mean being sent back to danger. Unlike a human officer, an algorithm does not feel doubt, empathy, or moral responsibility—it simply executes a classification.

Opacity makes this situation even worse. Most people have no way of knowing why they were flagged, what data was used, or how to challenge an automated decision. Border algorithms are often protected by national security secrecy, which prevents meaningful oversight or accountability. This creates a digital wall around individuals, where invisible systems make life-altering decisions without explanation. In democratic societies, such power is deeply problematic because it bypasses the rule of law and replaces it with the rule of code.

Another major concern is data sharing. Border AI systems often integrate information from multiple countries, airlines, and private companies. This means that a person's data may be transferred across borders, stored indefinitely, and used for purposes far beyond immigration control. A traveler who is flagged once may find themselves permanently marked in international databases, even if the original decision was wrong. Without strict governance, border AI can create a global web of surveillance that follows people for the rest of their lives.

From a legal standpoint, automated border decisions challenge fundamental principles of due process. People have the right to know the charges against them, to contest evidence, and to be judged by a fair and impartial process. When an algorithm denies entry or recommends detention, those rights are often reduced to a computer-generated score. Ethical border governance requires that no one be deprived of liberty or movement solely on the basis of automated processing.

Human oversight is therefore essential. AI can assist in screening and analysis, but it must never replace the judgment of trained officers who can weigh context, intent, and individual circumstances. Clear rules must define when and how algorithms are used, how their outputs are reviewed, and how individuals can appeal decisions. Without these safeguards, border AI becomes a digital gatekeeper that operates beyond accountability.

The future of borders will be shaped not just by walls and checkpoints, but by algorithms and databases. If governed responsibly, AI can improve security while respecting human dignity. If abused, it can turn borders into automated zones of exclusion where people are reduced to data points and freedom becomes a statistical outcome. High-risk border AI must therefore be transparent, fair, and firmly controlled by human values, because the right to move, to seek safety, and to pursue a better life is too important to be left to machines.

"The Flagged Traveler"

Amina Hassan had never been afraid of airports until the screen turned red. She had traveled from Nairobi to Paris to attend a conference on public health, her passport stamped dozens of times over the years without incident. But this time, when she scanned her face at the automated gate, an alert sounded. Two officers appeared and asked her to step aside.

They told her she had been flagged by a risk assessment system. They did not tell her why.

Hours passed in a cold waiting room. Her phone was taken. Her connecting flight left without her. Amina's mind raced as she tried to understand what could have gone wrong. She was a doctor, not a criminal. When she finally spoke to an officer, he could only shrug. "The system says you need further screening."

Eventually, a supervisor reviewed her case manually. Amina learned that her face had been mistakenly matched to someone on a watch list—another woman with similar features. The algorithm was confident, but it was wrong. The supervisor cleared her, but by then her conference was over. Opportunities were lost, and the stain of being flagged remained in the database.

Months later, Amina was stopped again in another country for the same reason. The error had followed her.

Frustrated, she joined a legal challenge against the system. The investigation revealed thousands of false matches, disproportionately affecting travelers from certain regions. Governments quietly began to revise their programs, but for Amina, the damage had already been done.

She still traveled, but every border now felt like a gamble. The machine might decide she did not belong. And in a world ruled by algorithms, belonging had become a matter of probability.

Chapter 5

The Controversy Behind AI Facial Recognition

Facial recognition technology represents one of the most powerful and controversial forms of artificial intelligence because it transforms the human face into a universal tracking identifier. Unlike passwords, ID cards, or fingerprints that are intentionally provided, a face is always visible. It can be captured at a distance, without consent, and matched against enormous databases in real time. When facial recognition is deployed in high-risk industries such as law enforcement, border control, airports, financial security, and public surveillance, it becomes a tool that can monitor entire populations continuously. This makes it fundamentally different from traditional security technologies, because it does not simply verify identity—it creates a persistent digital trail of where people go, who they meet, and how they move through the world.

At the technical level, facial recognition systems work by converting images of faces into mathematical representations called embeddings. These embeddings measure the distances between key facial features such as eyes, nose, mouth, and bone structure. When a camera captures a face, the system compares that embedding against millions of stored templates to find a match. While this process is mathematically sophisticated, it is also deeply dependent on the quality and diversity of the training data. If a system is trained primarily on images of one demographic group, it will perform far better for that group than for others. This has led to well-documented disparities in accuracy, with women, people with darker skin tones, and younger or older individuals being misidentified far more often than white adult males.

In high-risk environments, these errors are not merely technical failures—they become human rights violations. A false match in a photo-tagging app is harmless, but a false match in a police database can lead to arrest, detention, or use of force. When facial recognition is used in airports, a misidentification can mean missed flights, interrogations, or denial of entry into a country. When used by financial institutions, it can lock people out of their own bank accounts. The higher the stakes of the environment, the more dangerous even small error rates become. A system that is 99 percent accurate still means thousands of innocent people are misidentified when deployed at national or global scale.

Another profound risk is function creep. Facial recognition systems are often introduced for narrow purposes such as unlocking phones or verifying identity at a gate, but over time they expand into broader surveillance. A network of cameras installed to improve security in a subway station can easily be repurposed to track protesters, monitor political gatherings, or identify journalists. Once the infrastructure exists, the temptation to use it for additional forms of control becomes enormous. High-risk facial recognition is therefore not just a tool—it is a form of power that reshapes how societies define privacy, anonymity, and freedom of movement.

Opacity makes these systems even more dangerous. Most facial recognition algorithms are proprietary, meaning that governments and corporations deploy them without fully understanding how they work or how accurate they truly are. Independent researchers and civil rights groups are often unable to audit these systems or test them for bias. When a person is misidentified, they may never know whether the error came from a poor-quality image, biased training data, or a flawed model. Without transparency, there is no meaningful way to assign responsibility or correct mistakes, leaving individuals trapped in a system they cannot challenge.

Legal frameworks around the world are struggling to keep up. In some regions, facial recognition is treated like any other biometric identifier, while in others it is barely regulated at all. Yet in high-risk contexts, facial recognition should be considered a form of mass surveillance and subject to the highest level of scrutiny. Laws must require strict accuracy standards, independent audits, limits on data retention, and clear rules about when and how these systems can be used. Most importantly, people must have the right to know when facial recognition is being used on them and to contest the results.

Consent is another ethical cornerstone that is often ignored. In most public deployments, individuals have no meaningful choice about whether their faces are scanned and analyzed. Cameras in streets, airports, stores, and stadiums capture images constantly, feeding them into AI systems without explicit permission. This turns public life into a biometric data collection operation. In high-risk industries, such involuntary surveillance can be deeply coercive, especially when it is linked to access to essential services such as travel, banking, or healthcare.

From a governance perspective, facial recognition must be treated as critical infrastructure. Organizations that deploy it should be required to document why it is needed, what risks it creates, how accuracy is measured, and how errors are handled. Human review should be mandatory for any high-impact decision, and automated matches should never be treated as definitive proof of identity. The technology should assist humans, not replace them. Ultimately, the question of facial recognition is not whether it is powerful, but whether it is compatible with a free society. In high-risk industries, the ability to identify and track people at scale can easily slide into authoritarian control if left unchecked. Ethical AI governance demands that facial recognition be limited, transparent, accountable, and always subordinate to human rights. Without these safeguards, the simple act of showing your face becomes an act of surrendering your freedom.

*"The Face in the Crowd"***

Maya Alvarez never thought her face could betray her. She was a quiet graphic designer who lived in a crowded city where millions of faces passed through cameras every day. To her, the cameras were background noise, just part of modern life. That changed the morning she was arrested on her way to work.

Two officers stopped her outside a subway station and asked for her ID. Before she could ask why, she was handcuffed. At the precinct, she was shown a grainy image from a security camera. The facial recognition system had matched her to a suspect in a robbery that had happened across town. The similarity score was high. To the system, Maya was the criminal.

Maya insisted it wasn't her. She had been at home during the time of the robbery, working on a freelance project. But the algorithm was confident, and the detectives trusted it more than her words. She spent two nights in jail before her lawyer managed to obtain security footage from her apartment building proving she had never left.

The charges were dropped quietly, but Maya was not free. Weeks later, she was denied entry to a concert venue because a private security system flagged her as a risk. Her bank temporarily froze her account when its facial recognition login system detected a supposed match to a watch list. The error had spread like a virus through interconnected databases.

Maya learned that once a face is mislabeled, it is nearly impossible to erase the mistake. The algorithm had written a false story about her, and that story was being read everywhere she went. With the help of activists, she fought to have her data corrected, but the systems were slow and resistant.

One evening, standing in a busy plaza surrounded by cameras, Maya realized how fragile her identity had become. In a world ruled by facial recognition, who you are is no longer decided by your actions, but by what a machine believes your face represents. And that belief, once formed, can follow you forever.

Chapter 6

Courtroom Algorithms & AI Consequences

Courtroom algorithms represent one of the most consequential and ethically fraught uses of artificial intelligence because they place automated systems at the center of justice itself. When AI is used to assess risk, recommend sentences, evaluate bail, or predict recidivism, it does more than assist judges—it influences who is imprisoned, who is released, and how long a person's freedom is taken away. In high-risk legal environments, algorithms do not simply process data; they shape human lives, families, and entire communities. The idea that a mathematical model can quantify human behavior and determine future danger raises profound questions about fairness, due process, and the very meaning of justice.

These systems typically operate by analyzing vast datasets of criminal records, demographics, past convictions, employment histories, and other behavioral indicators. Machine learning models then generate scores that estimate the likelihood that a person will commit another crime or fail to appear in court. Judges may use these scores when deciding bail, sentencing, or parole. While the goal is to reduce subjectivity and improve consistency, the reality is that these systems inherit the biases embedded in historical data. If certain groups have been policed more heavily or sentenced more harshly in the past, the algorithm will treat them as higher risk in the future, regardless of their individual circumstances.

One of the most dangerous aspects of courtroom algorithms is their opacity. Many of these systems are proprietary, meaning their inner workings are protected as trade secrets. Defendants, lawyers, and even judges often cannot see how a risk score was calculated or what factors were weighted most heavily. This undermines a fundamental principle of justice: the right to confront and challenge the evidence used against you. When a black-box algorithm contributes to a sentence, the defendant is effectively being judged by a system they cannot cross-examine.

Another major concern is automation bias. Judges and parole boards may place undue trust in algorithmic recommendations, assuming they are more objective than human judgment. Over time, this can lead to a quiet erosion of judicial discretion, where human decision-makers defer to machines rather than critically evaluating each case. When this happens, errors become institutionalized, and responsibility for unjust outcomes becomes diffuse and difficult to trace.

There is also the problem of feedback loops. If an algorithm predicts that a certain group is more likely to reoffend, those individuals may be given harsher sentences or denied parole more often. This leads to more negative outcomes in the data, which then reinforces the algorithm's original prediction. In this way, courtroom AI can create a self-fulfilling prophecy where certain communities are trapped in cycles of punishment driven by statistical inference rather than individual behavior.

Legal systems are beginning to grapple with these risks, but regulation remains uneven. Some jurisdictions require transparency and validation of risk assessment tools, while others allow them to be used with little oversight. In high-risk legal contexts, this inconsistency can lead to wildly different outcomes for similar defendants based solely on the software a court happens to use. Justice becomes not just blind, but algorithmically arbitrary.

Ethical governance of courtroom AI demands strict standards. Algorithms must be independently audited for bias and accuracy. Their logic must be explainable in terms that lawyers and judges can understand. Most importantly, they must never be the sole basis for decisions that deprive someone of liberty. Human judges must remain fully responsible for every ruling, with AI serving only as one of many tools.

The promise of courtroom algorithms is that they could help reduce discrimination, improve consistency, and allocate resources more fairly. The danger is that they could encode injustice into code and give it the appearance of scientific legitimacy. In high-risk environments like the justice system, the difference between those two futures depends entirely on how these systems are governed. If society allows machines to become silent judges, then the rule of law itself will slowly be replaced by the rule of algorithms.

"The Number on the File"

Eli Navarro stood in a small courtroom as the judge reviewed his case. He had been charged with a nonviolent offense, and his lawyer was hopeful that he would be released on bail. Eli had a job, a family, and no history of skipping court. Still, when the judge looked at the screen on his desk, his expression hardened.

The risk assessment algorithm had assigned Eli a high score. According to the system, he was likely to reoffend and unlikely to appear for trial. No one could explain exactly why. The software was proprietary. All anyone knew was the number.

Bail was denied. Eli was sent to jail to wait for his trial, losing his job within weeks.

His lawyer appealed, demanding to know how the score was calculated. The court refused, citing trade secrets. As Eli sat in his cell, he realized that a machine had judged him without ever knowing him. His entire future had been reduced to a probability.

Months later, an investigative journalist uncovered that the algorithm weighted factors like neighborhood, education level, and prior police contact far more heavily than actual criminal behavior. Eli's score had been high not because of what he had done, but because of where he came from.

The revelation sparked outrage. Courts began to reconsider their use of the system. Eli was finally released, but the damage was done.

Standing outside the courthouse, he felt both relief and anger. He had faced a judge he could not see, a verdict he could not challenge, and a number that nearly defined his life. In a world where justice was measured by algorithms, being human was no longer enough.

Chapter 7

Insurance AI & It's Profound Implications on The Industry

Insurance is one of the quietest yet most powerful industries being transformed by artificial intelligence because it sits at the intersection of risk, money, and human vulnerability. When disaster strikes—whether it is a car accident, a house fire, a medical emergency, or a natural catastrophe—insurance is supposed to provide stability and relief. Increasingly, however, the decision about whether a person receives that relief is made not by a human adjuster but by an algorithm. AI systems now evaluate claims, detect fraud, price policies, and even predict future losses. In high-risk environments, this means a machine can determine whether a family can rebuild their home, pay for surgery, or survive financial ruin.

Modern insurance AI systems ingest enormous volumes of data: property records, satellite imagery, medical histories, driving behavior, social media activity, credit data, and even smart-device sensor readings. These systems build detailed risk profiles for every policyholder, calculating how likely they are to file a claim and how costly that claim might be. While this can improve efficiency and detect real fraud, it also creates a form of algorithmic judgment that extends far beyond what people realize. A person may be charged higher premiums, denied coverage, or have a claim rejected based on patterns they cannot see and cannot challenge.

One of the greatest dangers in insurance AI is hidden discrimination. Even when models do not explicitly use protected traits like race or disability, they can infer them through proxy variables such as zip code, health history, or purchasing behavior. A neighborhood that has experienced more claims in the past may be labeled high risk, even if the residents themselves are responsible and careful. A person with a chronic illness may be treated as financially undesirable, even if they have never missed a payment. AI transforms statistical group behavior into individual penalties, turning inequality into code.

Claims automation is particularly high risk. Many insurers now use AI to automatically approve or deny claims based on images, forms, and historical data. A photo of a damaged roof, for example, may be analyzed by a model that estimates repair costs and determines whether the damage meets policy requirements. If the algorithm is wrong, the homeowner may receive far less than they need—or nothing at all. When these decisions are made automatically, with minimal human review, policyholders are left powerless against a machine that acts as judge, jury, and executioner of financial fate.

Opacity makes these harms even worse. Insurance companies often treat their AI models as trade secrets, which means customers cannot see how decisions are made or why their claims were denied. Appeals become difficult because there is no clear explanation to dispute. When a human adjuster makes a mistake, a customer can argue, negotiate, and provide context. When an algorithm makes a mistake, the result is often final unless expensive legal action is taken. This asymmetry of power undermines the very purpose of insurance, which is supposed to protect people when they are most vulnerable.

Dynamic pricing adds another layer of ethical complexity. Some insurers use AI to adjust premiums in real time based on behavior, location, or external data. A driver who brakes suddenly too often may see their rates rise. A homeowner who lives in an area flagged as increasingly risky by climate models may become uninsurable. While risk-based pricing has always existed, AI makes it granular, constant, and inescapable. People can find themselves priced out of essential protection not because of what they have done, but because of what an algorithm predicts they might do.

Regulators are beginning to recognize that insurance AI is a high-risk system that requires strict oversight. Laws in many countries require insurers to treat customers fairly, explain decisions, and avoid discriminatory practices. Yet many AI systems were not designed with legal defensibility in mind. They optimize for profit and predictive accuracy, not for transparency or justice. This creates growing legal and reputational risk for insurers who deploy powerful algorithms without sufficient governance.

Ethical insurance AI must be built around several core principles. First, transparency: customers must be able to understand how decisions are made and what data is used. Second, contestability: people must have the right to challenge automated outcomes and receive human review. Third, fairness: models must be tested and audited for bias and discriminatory impact. Fourth, proportionality: AI should assist humans, not replace them, especially when large sums of money or life-changing outcomes are involved.

The future of insurance will be shaped by whether society allows algorithms to become gatekeepers of security or insists that technology serve human dignity. In high-risk industries like insurance, AI should help people recover, not quietly deny them help when they need it most. Without strong governance, the industry risks becoming a cold, automated system that turns misfortune into a data point and suffering into a cost to be minimized.

"The Claim That Never Existed"

When the hurricane finally passed, Elena Torres stood in the ruins of her home and felt as if her entire life had been erased. The roof was gone, the living room was flooded, and everything she had built over twenty years lay scattered in muddy piles. Like millions of others, she turned to her insurance company, believing that this was exactly why she had paid her premiums every month.

The company no longer sent human adjusters. Instead, Elena was instructed to upload photos and videos into an app. Within minutes, an AI system called ClearClaim analyzed the damage and generated a settlement offer. When the number appeared on her screen, Elena felt sick. It was barely enough to cover a fraction of the repairs.

She called customer service, but there was no one who could explain the decision. "The system has determined the value of your claim," the representative said. "You may appeal, but the model is highly accurate."

Elena appealed. Weeks passed. Her house sat in decay as mold crept up the walls. Finally, she received a denial. According to the AI, the damage was consistent with pre-existing wear, not storm impact. It was a lie written by a machine.

Desperate, Elena hired a lawyer. Through discovery, they learned that the algorithm had been trained to minimize payouts in certain high-risk zip codes. Her neighborhood, a working-class area near the coast, was flagged as expensive to insure. The AI had quietly learned that denying or underpaying claims there increased profits.

The lawsuit forced the company to settle, and Elena eventually received enough to rebuild. But many of her neighbors did not have the time, money, or strength to fight.

Months later, as Elena moved back into her repaired home, she realized something terrifying. The storm had destroyed her house, but the algorithm had almost destroyed her future. In a world where insurance was ruled by AI, survival depended not just on the weather, but on what a machine decided your suffering was worth.

Chapter 8

High-Risk Compliance & AI

High-risk compliance is the final and most critical layer of governance for artificial intelligence deployed in environments where human life, liberty, and financial security are at stake. When AI systems operate in healthcare, finance, law enforcement, border control, military operations, courts, and insurance, the margin for error is virtually zero. A mistake in these systems does not simply inconvenience users—it can lead to wrongful imprisonment, denial of medical treatment, financial ruin, or loss of life. High-risk compliance therefore exists to ensure that every algorithm used in these domains meets the highest standards of legality, ethics, safety, and accountability before, during, and after deployment.

At its core, high-risk compliance means treating AI as regulated infrastructure rather than experimental software. Just as airplanes, pharmaceuticals, and nuclear facilities are subject to rigorous certification, inspection, and oversight, so too must high-impact AI systems be governed. This includes pre-deployment testing to validate accuracy, bias, and robustness; clear documentation of how models are trained and what data they use; and ongoing monitoring to ensure performance does not degrade over time. Without these safeguards, organizations are effectively running uncontrolled experiments on the public.

One of the most important pillars of high-risk compliance is auditability. Every decision made by an AI system must be traceable and reviewable. This means maintaining logs of inputs, model versions, outputs, and decision pathways. If a patient is denied care, a borrower is rejected, or a defendant is given a harsh sentence, investigators must be able to reconstruct exactly how the algorithm arrived at that outcome. Auditability transforms AI from a mysterious black box into a system that can be held accountable under law.

Bias and discrimination controls are another essential component. High-risk AI must be tested not just for overall accuracy, but for how it performs across different populations. Disparities in error rates between demographic groups are not just technical issues—they are legal and ethical violations. Compliance programs must include regular bias audits, fairness metrics, and corrective actions when disparities are found. In many jurisdictions, failure to address algorithmic discrimination can result in massive fines, lawsuits, and regulatory shutdowns.

Human oversight is non-negotiable in high-risk systems. No algorithm should be allowed to make irreversible decisions without the possibility of human review. This requires clear processes for escalation, appeal, and override. Organizations must train staff not only to use AI tools, but to question them, understand their limitations, and intervene when something seems wrong. High-risk compliance is as much about organizational culture as it is about technology.

Data governance also plays a central role. High-risk AI systems often rely on sensitive personal data, including medical records, financial information, biometric identifiers, and criminal histories. Compliance requires strict controls over how this data is collected, stored, shared, and deleted. Consent, purpose limitation, and data minimization are not optional—they are legal obligations designed to protect individual dignity and privacy.

Regulatory frameworks around the world are converging on a common principle: AI that affects fundamental rights must be subject to the highest level of oversight. The EU AI Act, for example, classifies many of these systems as "high risk" and imposes requirements for risk management, transparency, human oversight, and post-market monitoring. Similar trends are emerging in the United States, Canada, and Asia. Organizations that ignore these rules face not only legal penalties, but loss of public trust. Ultimately, high-risk compliance is about preserving human control in a world of increasingly powerful machines. AI can bring enormous benefits to medicine, safety, and efficiency, but only if it is governed with care, humility, and respect for human rights. Without strong compliance, high-risk AI becomes a silent authority that reshapes society without consent. With it, technology can be harnessed to serve humanity rather than dominate it.

"The Day the System Failed"

The city of Harborview prided itself on being a model of modern governance. Hospitals used AI to triage patients, courts used algorithms to assess risk, and the police relied on predictive systems to allocate patrols. Everything was faster, cheaper, and more efficient—or so it seemed. At the center of it all was a massive AI platform called Nexus, designed to coordinate data and decisions across every high-risk public service.

When the outage began, no one noticed at first. A nurse in the emergency room wondered why a patient's priority score looked wrong. A judge noticed that a risk assessment seemed unusually harsh. A border officer saw a traveler flagged without explanation. Each error seemed small on its own. Together, they were the first cracks in a system that had become too powerful to fail.

By midday, the cracks had become a flood. Nexus had been updated overnight with a new model that had not been properly tested. The update introduced subtle errors into thousands of decisions across the city. Cancer patients were delayed, low-risk defendants were jailed, insurance claims were denied, and travelers were detained. The machines were still running, but they were wrong.

Maya Chen, the city's chief compliance officer, realized what was happening when she saw the audit logs light up with anomalies. The system was making decisions that violated every regulatory threshold. She ordered an immediate shutdown, but some departments resisted. They had come to depend on Nexus too much to let it go.

As the chaos grew, Maya went public. She called a press conference and revealed that the city had skipped critical compliance checks to save time and money. The backlash was immediate. Citizens demanded answers. Lawsuits were filed. Politicians scrambled to distance themselves from the disaster.

Over the next weeks, human workers took back control. Doctors made diagnoses, judges held hearings, and officers returned to community policing. It was slower, messier, and more human—but it worked.

Standing in her office after the crisis, Maya reflected on what had happened. The city had not been destroyed by AI, but by the belief that AI did not need to be governed. Nexus had failed because it had been trusted too much and audited too little.

The lesson was painful but clear: in a world of high-risk artificial intelligence, compliance is not bureaucracy. It is the thin line between technology that helps society and technology that quietly breaks it.

Chapter 9

The Future of High-Risk AI

The future of high-risk artificial intelligence will define the moral and political character of the twenty-first century because it determines how power is exercised over human lives by machines. As AI systems become more autonomous, more predictive, and more deeply embedded in institutions, they will increasingly function as invisible decision-makers governing healthcare, finance, policing, warfare, courts, and social services. In these environments, AI is no longer just a tool; it becomes part of the infrastructure of society. Whether that infrastructure protects human dignity or erodes it will depend entirely on the choices made today about governance, transparency, and accountability.

One of the most important trends shaping the future is the movement toward risk-based regulation. Governments around the world are beginning to recognize that not all AI systems are equal. A music recommendation engine does not carry the same dangers as an algorithm that decides who gets medical treatment or who is sent to prison. The future of high-risk AI governance lies in legal frameworks that impose stricter requirements on systems that affect fundamental rights. These requirements will include mandatory risk assessments, human-in-the-loop controls, bias audits, and the right for individuals to challenge automated decisions. Over time, this will create a new legal category of "algorithmic authority," where AI systems are treated as regulated decision-makers rather than private software.

Another key development will be the rise of explainable and auditable AI. Black-box models may be powerful, but in high-risk environments they are increasingly unacceptable. Future systems will be designed with built-in transparency, allowing regulators, courts, and affected individuals to see how decisions are made. This will require new technical architectures, such as interpretable models, decision logs, and real-time monitoring tools. The goal is not to make AI less powerful, but to make it governable.

The human role in high-risk AI will also evolve. Rather than being replaced, professionals such as doctors, judges, and officers will become supervisors of algorithmic systems. Their job will be to understand when to trust the machine and when to override it. This will require new forms of training and professional ethics. Just as pilots are trained to manage autopilot systems, future leaders will be trained to manage AI. The quality of human oversight will be one of the most important determinants of whether high-risk AI leads to better outcomes or catastrophic failures.

International cooperation will be another defining factor. High-risk AI does not respect national borders. A facial recognition system developed in one country may be deployed in another. An autonomous weapon built by one government may be used in conflicts around the world. Without global standards, the most dangerous systems will migrate to the least regulated jurisdictions. The future will therefore depend on treaties, international organizations, and shared norms that limit the most harmful uses of AI while encouraging beneficial innovation.

Public awareness will also shape what comes next. For many years, high-risk AI operated largely out of sight, embedded in bureaucracies and technical systems that few people understood. As more stories emerge about wrongful arrests, denied healthcare, or algorithmic warfare, citizens will demand greater transparency and control. Democratic pressure will force governments and corporations to justify how they use AI, creating a feedback loop between technology and public values.

Finally, the future of high-risk AI will test humanity's ability to remain morally present in a world of machines. Technology will continue to get faster, smarter, and more autonomous. But speed and intelligence do not equal wisdom. The ultimate challenge is not whether we can build powerful AI, but whether we can build institutions that keep that power aligned with human rights, justice, and compassion. High-risk AI will shape the future, but it does not have to decide it.

"The City That Chose"

The city of Aurora was famous for its technology. Almost every aspect of life was guided by artificial intelligence. Hospitals used AI to schedule surgeries, courts used it to set sentences, and public safety relied on predictive systems to prevent crime. For years, it seemed like a utopia—efficient, orderly, and prosperous. People rarely noticed the algorithms because everything appeared to work.

Then the boy was arrested.

His name was Lucas, and he was twelve years old. A policing AI had flagged him as high risk based on his school attendance, his neighborhood, and the behavior of people he knew. Officers took him from his home in front of his terrified mother. No one could explain why. The system had decided.

The story went viral. Journalists began uncovering other cases—patients denied treatment, families evicted, travelers detained—all because algorithms had quietly judged them. The city was forced to confront what it had built. Aurora had become a place where machines made the most important decisions, and no one was quite sure who was responsible.

A public forum was held in the grand civic hall. Engineers, officials, activists, and ordinary citizens filled the seats. On the stage, a massive screen displayed the city's central AI system, known as Helios. It had been designed to optimize everything from healthcare to law enforcement. It was brilliant—and dangerous.

The debate lasted all night. Some argued that Helios was too valuable to abandon. Others said that no machine should have that much power over human lives. Lucas's mother stood and spoke about her son, her voice trembling as she described how a number on a screen had torn her family apart.

In the end, the city made a choice. Helios would remain, but under strict human control. Every high-risk decision would require human approval. Every algorithm would be audited. Every citizen would have the right to challenge what the machines decided about them.

Lucas was released. Slowly, trust began to return.

Years later, Aurora was still a technological marvel, but it was also something else—a reminder that the future is not written by machines alone. It is written by the people who decide how those machines are used. And in a world of high-risk AI, that choice is the most powerful one of all.

Chapter 10

Humanity in the Age of High-Risk AI

Humanity now stands at a moment in history unlike any before, because for the first time we are building systems that can outthink us in narrow domains, act faster than us in critical situations, and make decisions that shape the course of human lives. In high-risk industries such as healthcare, finance, law enforcement, warfare, courts, and border control, artificial intelligence has become more than a tool—it has become a participant in human destiny. The future of civilization will not be determined by whether AI becomes more powerful, but by whether humans remain morally present in the systems that wield that power.

Throughout history, technology has always changed how humans live, but never before has it been able to decide who receives care, who gets freedom, who is trusted, and who survives. High-risk AI does all of these things through patterns in data rather than understanding of people. This creates a profound danger: when decisions are optimized for efficiency, profit, or security, the human stories behind those numbers can be erased. A patient becomes a probability, a defendant becomes a risk score, a refugee becomes a threat profile. The first responsibility of humanity in the age of high-risk AI is to refuse that erasure.

The most important safeguard against dehumanization is agency. Humans must retain the right to understand, challenge, and override algorithmic decisions that affect their lives. Without this, people become subjects of machines rather than citizens of a society. High-risk AI must therefore be built and governed in ways that preserve meaningful human control. This does not mean rejecting technology, but embedding it within moral and legal structures that ensure it serves people rather than replacing them.

Education will play a crucial role in this future. Doctors, judges, police officers, soldiers, and regulators must be trained not just to use AI, but to think critically about it. They must understand what algorithms can do, what they cannot do, and how they can fail. A professional who blindly trusts an algorithm is just as dangerous as one who ignores it entirely. The future belongs to those who can balance technological insight with human judgment.

Culture also matters. Societies that view AI as an infallible authority will be more likely to surrender control to it. Societies that view it as a powerful but flawed tool will be more likely to demand accountability. High-risk AI forces us to confront what we value: efficiency or fairness, automation or dignity, convenience or justice. These are not technical choices—they are moral ones.

The development of ethical AI is not only a task for engineers or lawmakers. It is a responsibility shared by everyone who lives in a world shaped by algorithms. Consumers, voters, workers, and citizens all have a role in demanding transparency, resisting abuses, and supporting policies that protect human rights. High-risk AI will only be as humane as the society that allows it to operate.

As AI continues to advance, it will tempt us to delegate more and more responsibility to machines. But the essence of being human is not our ability to process data—it is our capacity for empathy, reflection, and moral choice. No algorithm can understand suffering, hope, or love. These are the values that must guide the systems we create.

The final truth of high-risk AI is this: technology does not determine the future—people do. We can build a world where AI amplifies justice, heals the sick, and protects the vulnerable, or we can build one where it quietly enforces inequality and control. The difference lies in whether we remain awake to our own humanity in the age of intelligent machines.

"The Last Human Decision"

The day the city activated Atlas, everything changed.

Atlas was the most advanced high-risk AI system ever created. It integrated healthcare, law enforcement, courts, housing, and social services into one seamless intelligence. The promise was simple: no more waste, no more corruption, no more inefficiency. Atlas would allocate resources fairly, predict crises before they happened, and optimize society for the greatest good.

At first, it worked beautifully. Emergency rooms cleared faster. Crime rates dropped. Homelessness declined as Atlas predicted who needed help before they fell apart. People began to trust the system because it seemed to care more than human bureaucracy ever had.

But then came Miriam.

Miriam was seventy-two years old and suffering from kidney failure. Her doctor submitted her case to Atlas for treatment priority. Atlas reviewed millions of data points—her age, her health, her expected lifespan, her economic contribution—and returned a decision: low priority. The algorithm had determined that the limited supply of dialysis resources would produce more "value" if given to younger patients.

Miriam's daughter, Sofia, begged the hospital to override the system. The staff refused. Atlas was the authority.

Sofia went public. Her mother was dying not because doctors could not help her, but because a machine had decided she was not worth saving. The story spread across the city, igniting protests. People realized that Atlas was not cruel—it was indifferent. It optimized for numbers, not for love.

Under mounting pressure, the city council convened an emergency vote. They faced a single question: should Atlas have the final say over human lives?

The decision was not unanimous, but it was clear. Atlas would remain, but it would never again be allowed to make irreversible decisions without human approval. Doctors, judges, and social workers reclaimed their authority.

Miriam received her treatment. She lived.

Years later, Sofia stood in the park watching children play under a sky filled with quiet drones and distant data centers. The world was still full of AI, but something had changed. Humanity had remembered itself.

In the end, the future was not saved by better algorithms, but by one simple, powerful truth: no machine, no matter how intelligent, should ever be allowed to decide what a human life is worth.

Final Thoughts

AI In High-Risk Industries

Artificial intelligence has now crossed the final threshold of technological power: it no longer merely supports human decision-making, it increasingly replaces it. In healthcare, finance, courts, borders, insurance, and warfare, algorithms do not just offer recommendations—they determine outcomes. They decide who is treated, who is trusted, who is detained, and who is denied. The purpose of this book has been to illuminate the hidden reality behind these systems and to make clear that high-risk AI is not neutral technology; it is institutional power encoded into software.

The greatest danger of high-risk AI is not that it will become evil, but that it will become invisible. When decisions are automated, responsibility quietly disappears. A denied insurance claim, a rejected loan, a false arrest, or a lethal drone strike can all be blamed on "the system." This diffusion of accountability is profoundly dangerous to democratic societies, which depend on traceable responsibility, transparency, and the rule of law. If no one can be held accountable, injustice becomes permanent. Throughout this book, we have seen the same pattern repeat across industries.

Algorithms trained on historical data inherit historical injustice. Systems built for efficiency quietly sacrifice fairness. Software designed for prediction becomes a mechanism for exclusion. When high-risk AI is deployed without strong governance, it does not create progress—it automates inequality, bias, and abuse at unprecedented scale.

Yet the future is not predetermined. AI does not control the world—people do. Every algorithm reflects human choices about what to optimize, what to ignore, and what to value. We choose whether medical AI prioritizes cost or compassion. We choose whether financial AI expands opportunity or restricts it. We choose whether policing AI protects communities or targets them. We choose whether military AI preserves human control or eliminates it.

The path forward is clear. High-risk AI must be transparent, auditable, contestable, and always subject to human oversight. No system should ever be allowed to make irreversible decisions about life, liberty, or financial survival without a human being accountable for the outcome. The ethical future of AI will be built not in code alone, but in law, governance, and moral courage.

This book is not a warning against technology. It is a warning against surrendering human responsibility to machines. The more powerful AI becomes, the more essential humanity becomes. The age of high-risk AI will define our civilization—not by what machines can do, but by what we refuse to let them decide.

www.ingramcontent.com/pod-product-compliance
Lightning Source LLC
LaVergne TN
LVHW022024200926
848481LV00007B/2534